Spare Parts

Cover Painting: Papa's '37 Jimmy
© 2003 Duane Hada

MONGREL EMPIRE PRESS
NORMAN, OKLAHOMA, UNITED STATES OF AMERICA

WWW.MONGRELEMPIREPRESS.COM

This publisher is a proud member of

[clmp]

COUNCIL OF LITERARY MAGAZINES & PRESSES
w w w . c l m p . o r g

Founding Member

OKLAHOMA
SMALL PRESS
ASSOCIATION

Book Design: Mongrel Empire Press using iWork Pages.

Spare Parts

POEMS BY

Ken Hada

MONGREL EMPIRE PRESS   NORMAN, OK

Acknowledgments

Some of the poems in this collection first appeared in:

California Quarterly
Exit 109: A Poetry and Prose Anthology
Homestead Review
Kansas City Voices
Looking Back: A Poetry and Prose Anthology
Many Mountains Moving
RE:AL
The Mid-America Poetry Review

for Kenny

Contents

x

Someone said that when we go before the judge we should tell him that spare parts commit no sins. That's what we are, life's spare parts. And while we're alive, shouldn't life at least be kind to us?

—Yasunari Kawabata
The Sound of the Mountain

First Attempts at Killing

The BB gun came with a rule:
Don't shoot songbirds,
Robins, Cardinals and those kind.
You can shoot Sparrows.

Something did not seem right
but two sun-tanned boys
nodded *OK* and gulped
at thoughts of trigger squeezing.

The first target soon lit:
a Robin on a fencepost.
The elder brother aimed the gun
then a short discussion

Regarding the rule – failed –
the way all rules seem
unclear, unconvincing
when blood and lust engage.

He aimed again, fired –
the bird fell flopping in dust.
An imperfect shot
left them sick but well

On their way toward learning
to justify behavior:
hiding and spinning things
that should never be hidden or spun.

Games I Used To Play

At first it was a sawmill slab
I swung as a bat
cracking round hard rocks
high and deep to the treeline,
the imagined wall of Busch Stadium.

Then I used my Louisville Slugger,
cracked as it was from real baseball,
it was the perfect instrument
to project my fantasy
to Major League level.

I'd play nine innings
going through the lineup of each team
imitating stances of every player
talking the microphone talk
building the sport within me, about me.

I knew both satisfaction
and sadness when the final out occurred.
I would carry my rock-riddled bat
over my shoulder, walking home
with the familiar gait of one

Who knows winning and losing
striding along toward supper
all the while believing
I was that much closer to something
I could only imagine.

That pretense was real then
but the only thing true
was the commitment I made
and the unspoken reasons
why such commitment was needed.

Dad's Sled

He built it with used two by fours
scrap metal for runners.
He always saved spare parts

and cast-off material.
We might use that someday
he would say – and sure enough,

one day when the ice and snow came,
the Old Bailey Hill beckoned.
I stood beside him

in the cold basement as he framed
a sled from a design
tucked away in his memory.

I helped by holding the wood
in place as he nailed it tight,
then tacked on the runners.

We rode that sled every day
the cold lasted, screaming with delight
flying downhill in home-made ecstasy.

But today I remember the making
of the sled. It is in building
that his genius lay, and how I marvel

at his ability to make happiness
out of things left over, used
and otherwise abandoned.

Erasing

*Only the hand that erases
can write the true thing.*
— *Meister Eckhart*

Do you remember the power
you held in your hand
in first grade,
the ability to make false marks
disappear,
the satisfaction gained
by turning the pencil on its head
and stroking mistakes
until they were dust
to blow away,
and do you remember
placing your fingers over the spot
you had just erased
sensing the smooth whiteness
of a page reclaimed?

Then you knew
that learning to write
meant learning to write
again.

Empty Barrel

When I was a boy
I played with a blue
fifty-gallon barrel.

I passed time
making up games
drumming, listening
rolling downhill.

I remember hollow
thumping most,
gonging sounds
rising from emptiness
speaking to me.

It still does.

Murmurings

Driving slow past
the old Duvall place
we hushed our voices,
weeds clamoring above window sills

torn screens flapping
front door hanging ajar
rusty fence sagging
Devil's Tongue sibilating at dusk.

Creeping along gravel
panicking under the car wheels
Mom, with a gleam haunting
her eye, would whisper

the story of Mrs. Duvall
one dark lonely night
chopping her drunk man
to pieces with a splitting maul.

Nobody ever knew
what happened to the axing lady,
but that didn't stop
the telling or believing.

Disappearing into peccant air
she went home
to the Devil,
but she could always come back.

Witch weed and Snakeroot
murmuring in twilight
I gripped the back of my neck
each time we passed.

Baptism

In Bear Creek

under the railroad trestle
in our favorite swimming hole

we sang hymns,
mom playing the accordion.

Dad said a prayer
then took my hand

waded me deep
into the transparent stream,

minnows scurrying
and crawdads retreating

as we shuffled
toward the right place.

Frigid water pressing
my ebullient heart

I stood shivering
in holy water.

Dad put his white hanky
firm on my nose

looked up into bright sun,
said the words

and pushed my head under.

A Tentative Boy

lies late in a fearful night
hearing mother tell father
to kill himself.

Just kill yourself.
Drive your truck off a bluff somewhere
and don't come home
tomorrow.

The moon strikes the windowpane,
a pale gleam carving
the child into latticework
of shadow and light.

Stringing Fish

It is important that you learn
how to string a fish.

You must get it right the first time:
insert the shaft into the gaping mouth

without dropping the flopping
wet fish (no excuse will do).

Pull the shaft through the gill
or lower lip then push it back through

the loop, then secure the stringer
to a big rock or a tree limb.

If you do it wrong it means you
are still a boy, that you have quite

a bit to learn and a long way to go
before you are a man.

Driving

After driving miles and hours
I pull over to stretch
close my eyes
and see dad stopping the Olds

Getting out
standing at the hood
hands on his pockets.

I'm seven or eight.

I get out to stand
with him.

Mom is helling
inside the car
trapped
in mania
indescribable
unforgettable.

Clouds fill the afternoon.
I don't remember a sunset,
another fucked up family picnic.

Dad looks far off
and I try to follow
the path of his gaze,
try to help him
see a way out.

What do I know?

What can we do?

How love binds
to the point of breaking
even good boys
who just want peace
who just want to know
how to solve her
anger, her terror,
herself.

We did not know then
that some things
cannot be helped.

I open my eyes
and feel strange hope,
flex my arms,
climb back in the driver's seat.

These miles ahead
sometimes seem too much
like the miles behind –
those miles – driving
all these days.

A Carpenter's Son

He lives with the knowledge
of his limited skill,
rough, unfinished,
apprentice for life.

The wood of his crafting
bears marks of mishandled tools,
confesses imprecise strokes,
miscalculations –

A rough copy of the master
but imitation nonetheless.

Bowling Alley

When you grow up in the country
going to town is a ceremony.

As a kid you went to town for a haircut
and a piece of bubble gum

or to carry the milk to the car
or buy feed while parents mysteriously

paid bills or found you a new pair
of shoes – Saturday sidewalks full

of similar quests. But one place
was different – on the fringe of town

outlined in neon, beer signs flashing
– dark and smoky – spooky.

You somehow knew your destiny
was to one day borrow the car

take a friend or two to town
on Saturday night – circle the square

eat at the Sonic, then go
to the bowling alley, to the place

where you dared not be a dork, where
ruckus music could spark kissing

or fights in the parking lot –
your turn in a cycle of freedom

you feared and craved – just a step
or two above shooting rifles at stop signs.

Cathedral in the Grass

She sits cross-legged
under yellow grass that stands
belly-high to a horse
in a field far enough away
where a parent could not hear giggles,
could not see him crouched
on nine-year-old knees
looking reverently
at her shining auburn hair.

Afternoon shadows lengthen
across her, wrap around
to her pink mouth and hazel eyes
gleaming at his squeamishness
while keeping watch
on their favorite place to hide.

Looking back, he hopes only
to be forgiven
for *not* worshiping.

Pancake Nights

Shadows fall unnoticed outside.
We try to contain our home-made joy
without disturbing mom
who lies trapped in her bedroom shadows.

At the kitchen stove Dad sings,
mixing batter, refereeing an eating contest.
We are too poor to eat better,
too hungry to know the difference.

We top some with margarine
and cheap syrup, some with plum
or blackberry jelly, some
with generic brand peanut butter.

Our stomachs fill, Dad's singing lulls
as he washes dishes alone
looking out the kitchen window
into those long evening shadows.

Candelabra

I remember a candelabra
with spinning angels twirling
above four white flames
that pushed the chiming blades
on their circular route --
shadows silhouetted on the ceiling.

I remember a mother
celebrating her family's advent --
dad sitting in the big chair,
all of us kids at home
sitting around a worn coffee table
on the used sofa.

God was in that candelabra --
chiming the voice of approval.

New Year's Eve

We load the dogs into the back of the green dodge
and pile in beside them digging our faces
into the lining of their bellies to keep warm
as dad drives us down a snowy logging trail
into the icy hollows for one last coon hunt.

With numb fingers we unleash the dogs,
they bolt from the frozen truck bed seeking blood
their breaths blowing heat of the kill.
We follow them with fierce frivolity
over ice gripped rock through dormant timber.

We hear their baying way up in front of us
somewhere in the blackness.
We maraud under the white hot stars
until our lungs burn,
our teary eyelids freeze.

We know somewhere the dark river waits for us,
its chilling power coming into focus.
The dogs tree on the other side,
bright stars smirk at our dilemma
while we seek the courage to cross.

We decide. We undress to the naked bone
and step into the icy current
our groins wrenching in pain,
appendages recoiling toward atrophy
we snail our way along.

Numb feet slipping across mossy rock
sharp gravel lodging between our toes
reminding us of our limited nature,
still we move forward
trying not to betray our eager hounds.

Heads down seeking equilibrium
we creep through the cryptic river
against the deepening current
toward the other side
to satisfy the chase.

Half way across we hear splashing,
raise our heads to meet our dogs returning
sulking toward us.
We pause as timeless things
in bitter water.

Embarrassed to return without quarry,
fearing the dark current
we follow our subdued hounds back
crawling along the river bed
shivering like failures.

Then we hear cracking limbs in flames.
We look up to find dad's bonfire
blazing, reassuring
welcoming us out of the cold dark,
the old year ending.

Dominos

A quiet understanding between us
keeps order, makes us love
what we don't always like.

I no longer remind him
of failure and he never speaks
of disappointment.

He turns the spinner,
sighs and knows what plays
he has caused.

He doesn't block the game
every hand, but every hand
forces me to consider

limited moves,
playful options disguised
in ivory-coated dots

clicking between us –
that joy of the game
sounding so much more
so much more.

Questions

Questions arise out of nowhere:
like the time he found a condom
in dad's top drawer
was he twelve or eleven—
and was it really what he thought it must be
how could mystery packaged so tightly
laying beside shoe strings and hankies
in a drawer stuffed with tee shirts and briefs
be the same token of shame
he had discovered laying in the church parking lot
used and devilish
how could the thing signal the same kind of union
between estranged and forlorn parents
as it meant to those frivolous teens
who upon coming to a decision
laughed with guilty pleasure
discarded the semen-filled balloon
on to holy ground
before driving away into night
tail-lights simmering in darkness?

Ancestors

Once you shook the dust off them
you found hard men
driven in their denial
of fear, of failure.

They preferred plowing to killing
but there weren't many options
once they pissed off the czar
and his army.

They found a boat headed
for New York, found
a prairie home and tried to keep it
living on cabbage and coffee.

They worked and died young
but I'd like to think they died free.
They believed in the freedom
of dirt, turning sod,

Turning possibility over and over
every spade-full a chance,
every chance
the reprieve of destiny.

Grandpa Elmer

At five I sat on his lap in his rocking chair
watching the sun wake up over the horizon.

At seven he joked from his hospital bed
about the stitching scarred across his heart.

At seventeen I saw red roses and yellow wheat
grown in his field draped across his coffin.

He lay in a black suit with his hands folded across
his lap and a smile set in place, but I think he

should have been buried in blue, striped overalls
with CeeTee pliers in his grip and an Old Timer

knife in his pocket. We stood around the pink
granite stone in the cold wind to say goodbye.

I held tight his pocket watch. Sometimes when
I feel cold wind, I open that watch and think

about the sun rising and grave granite stones.

That Evening

that evening

    after the service
    after the casket

was lowered into red dirt
dirt which he had plowed
and planted

    I sat with her
    in the house

a house that would never be
the same, the house of grandkids
and trophies from prize quilts
and blue-ribbon jams from
county fairs

    and she spoke some
    and I spoke some

I was not yet eighteen
He was sixty five

    so my thoughts
    too few memories

the shotgun he bought for me
at auction, catching a big bass
on his cane pole, sitting on his lap
at sunrise, hearing growls about
harvest and calves, hay, tractors
and fences

now it would all change
we both knew that

as we sat holding our differing
grief, it would all change

some for the better
but not all

sundown and death – too obvious
to construct – that first night
was hard, but she was hard too

and she teaches me
to live on

for thirty more years (and counting)
that evening still alive in me –
a lesson in grief

believe it, bear it
bury it

When I was a Texan

I remember a yellow trailer loaded
behind the station wagon
we left Arkansas at night—
a balmy windy night—
and when I woke up we were in a place
called Texas—South Oak Cliff Dallas—
 and I don't know why

I went to kindergarten at Harold Bud
Elementary—mom taught me to tie my shoes
before I bravely marched two blocks to school
I don't remember much else

I don't remember the teacher's name,
 don't remember her face
don't remember the kids

except

there was a black boy I remember
who always shook his leg real fast in class
never seen a black boy before in north Arkansas

I remember walking home with black and brown boys,
stopping to eat tortillas at the Mexican lady's
house on the corner. I didn't know what a Mexican was
she didn't speak, she smiled and gave us tortillas,
I didn't know what tortillas were but I
usually took a second one rolled in butter

at Christmas mom and dad tricked me onto
the porch to see if it had snowed, if there would be a white
Christmas in South Oak Cliff Dallas—
I got a golden bike that would become my palomino—
I was a cowboy from the start

I learned to ride in South Oak Cliff Dallas
dad pushed me and I wobbled, but I pedaled hard
I have wobbled some since,
but I have never stopped pedaling

one day dad came home from the factory and told about a man
shot—gunned to death on the street in South Oak Cliff Dallas

then

we moved to the White Rock Lake area
and rented a nice big house
and everyone around us was white
and I went into third grade
and Craig Morton was my hero

except

the neighborhood quarterback never let me be
Craig Morton since he really got to go to Cowboy
games but mom bought me shoulder pads
at a garage sale —then I was Craig Morton and
Bob Lilly and Bobby Hays and anybody else
I wanted to be

until

a truck ran over my football on Marsalis avenue
and mom started crying everyday
wanting to go back to Arkansas—she cried
and sang a song about Arkansas and cried

until

we moved back and that is all that happened
to me in Texas

until

I fell in love with a senorita from McAllen
and I tried real hard to learn *la lengua*
and kissed all the aunts and ate the chilies
and moved to '*La Valle*' to become *hijo en la familia*

until

I began to miss the orange leaves in October
and noticed the absence of Dogwoods in April,
and I thought about leaving

until

my son was born down there
and I knew my life would always be down there
I crossed the bridge—fished in *Laguna Madre*
and decided I would always be *un hijito*

hasta

I got divorced and my son couldn't live in two places
so I headed *al norte* across the Red River
thinking I would never go back

the magic palms had frozen and they looked stupid
sticking upright with no leaves on them
I wanted a hurricane to blow them down
to change everything, to change me
so I took a gunny sack full of *naranjas* and walked away—
never think of the Rio Grande anymore

except

every October when a flock of geese honk in the night air
heading down Brownsville way

I came back
I crossed the Red River again
I located in the metroplex
I said it would only be temporary
I didn't want to go insane in the traffic on freeways
 that are not free, I breathed smog,
I longed for something green
I worked the graveyard shift on Christmas Eve
in the warehouse and wondered how I would ever get
back to wherever it was I was going
I heard about ladies getting cut up with knives
and heard about drug deals going bad and wondered
why *mis compadres* and I had to work in a warehouse on
Christmas Eve

I went to an apartment
and locked the door and spoke to no one
living in isolation
a metro man
hoping for only peace
pretending I was alive

until

the day was over
and I went back to the warehouse to load trucks
so the stockholders could get rich
so yuppies could supply themselves
so I could make rent
on the floor I slept

until

la musica de los mojados
working on their *carrito* woke me
I went outside to watch the giant birds
landing at DFW

I wondered about man
wondered how man could survive
when all he did was move
and make noise
and move somewhere else
perpetual motion

until

Dogwood

Brief flowers
teach me
your mountain secrets:

To flourish
in harshness
to flower
in shadows.

Pop Bottle Pete

He rode a red bicycle
pieced together from parts
found at the county dump,
fading paint, rusty spokes,
wrinkled basket on bent handle-bars.

He gathered discarded bottles,
finding them scattered along streets,
in trash bins, even taking them
out of your pickup bed.

He never smiled or frowned as he rode
peddling his bottles
five cents apiece at the market.

He never noticed drivers swerving,
children wondering.

Old Men

I make it a point now
to wave to old men I pass
old men standing in shade
of a yard, maybe
a daughter's place
where now he's just a tenant
trying to understand role reversal.

I raise my forefinger
as I steer country roads or pass
through tired neighborhoods.
Most return a wave or nod *Howdy*.
Driving gives you some perspective,
shows you how you might end up.

We allow something
now, especially those of us sitting
on porch swings, those
who never got around to going
somewhere, those
who still feel like something
somehow is missing.

Growing Pain

Those first moments
living alone
in your treehouse
we built,
grandpa and I and you
hammered a place
for your thoughts.

I see you standing
on the platform
high above it all
leaning safe
on supporting limbs
watching clouds
thinking as children think.

Now we live apart
in separate places:
I enjoy you
growing
celebrate your freedom
but also can't help but feel
something else.

Jack-O'-Lantern

I remember selecting pumpkins
with you, the choices mattered
the expectations you imagined.

I remember the knife, the big spoon
cleaning out the insides,
scraping the surface as dry as possible.

I remember your magic-markered drawings
and precise incisions following the lines
until a face emerged.

I remember lighting candles
then placing our paladins on the porch
after naming them.

I remember when fear was laughable
and the ghosts of winter
held no sway.

Yard Sale

A tattered lady stands the American flag
curbside, beside a large cardboard box
with the words YARD SALE magic-markered
in black, entrepreneurial lettering.

Two neighbors, side by side,
in two of the humblest homes in one
of the least prosperous parts of town
look over their displayed wares on the front lawn.

It's Saturday morning, not a cloud in sight,
an Autumn breeze bites just enough
to require a jacket as they wait
on what the day might bring them.

Have you made any money yet?
one calls to the other, interrupting the morning
perhaps to bolster anticipation.
Is this thrift? Capitalism? Or just a game?

What does the ritual of salvaging
and discarding mean? Who could want
or need *their* stuff? The neighbor answers:
Not yet. Not even one dollar.

Front Porch People

Barefoot in Texas, day two
of February, a south breeze
rises somewhere in the Gulf
swings inland all the way
past Austin to Temple

where cousins stomp
and strum guitar rhythms,
the porch swing keeping time.
Dusk approaches, friendly
dogs bark at the old neighbor

who picks up pecans,
leathered man living alone,
friend to trees and Gulf
breezes and white neighbors
picking homage

to *guitarreros* of old.
Ice tea glasses mostly empty
dinner plates splattered
with green salsa stains
scattered on a wood table.

No one wants to be inside
and miss evening bliss,
the rusty chains on the swing,
dusty siding waiting spring
rains. No one notices.

Music tempers the mood.
Across the street haphazard
flocks of grackles rise
into the south breeze.
I think they like friction

at their chests, making their
wings work harder,
like boys and guitars
strumming hard now.
We tap in time, nod along,

the dogs at attention.
El Viejo raises, cocks
his ear tuneward, grins.
Winter comforts
like summer's faint echo.

Everything depends on a guitar,
depends on a family,
barefoot, drunk on sweet tea
and the Muse
at Texas dusk.

Maypearl Texas

I saw him exiting the interstate
high-stepping like a rodeo pony.
He wore black boots, chaps, vest
blue denim shirt and, yes, a black hat.

He carried a suitcase
in his right hand, in the other
a guitar case plastered with stickers
announcing all the places he'd been.
He might've even played some of them.

He walked like he'd ridden a horse
before, I'll give him that.
He walked with a true gait
kind of a giddy up
and slow this thing down
at the same time – you know
the pattern – kind of like *Whoa boy!*
Take 'er easy partner
all the while gigging flank
and giving rein.
He knew how to walk in boots
and how to wear a hat.
That right there says something.

Like wild flowers growing
in the meridian, he is returning
and I bet he's got lots to tell.

Tacos in Denton

A Mexican lady in Denton
makes the best tacos.

She doesn't speak English
and her customers *By Gawd* can't talk *Meskin*.

They point past her shoulder
to the sign hanging beyond her above the grill

And say in a loud, girly voice:
Two Tacos Korneetus – yea those ones!

She nods and grins a modest grin
and things mostly work out for the best.

My Favorite White Trash Diner

These old gals' been rode hard
and put up wet
not a few times

Still you got to admire them

Their tip money becomes a new hairdo
or nails polished
or maybe a necklace or ring

Some have wedding rings,
reruns, but who's counting

They're awful open about love
or the lack thereof

Love is a good topic I guess
served with eggs

Breakfast makes us consider
what we might otherwise not get around to

They remember a time
when their beauty held more promise
but, by God,
they won't surrender to time
or anyone else, for that matter

Unless of course
there's hope to be gained

They smile a genuine smile
greet you loud and friendly
like a midway barker

They know
life is more than this –

But not much

If there was such a thing as justice
they'd be running this town

In a way they do
but it's a backhanded way

What they dream, how they cope
is nobody's damn business
except, of course, you ask
and they'll tell it

Whatever *It* is, for them
It is hidden in their hearts,
hearts broken and mended
like duct tape on leaky valves

And I wouldn't want to cross them
And I wouldn't want them crossed—again

I dig a good tip out of my wallet

I stack my plates
lay utensils across
pile used napkins and jelly packs on top

It is something – it is something
I feel compelled to do

Waitress

She'll be here twenty five
years from now because
she's good because she
refills your coffee without
asking because she takes
your order with a smile

Because she does not annoy

She'll be a lifetime here
because she's good
and because she's good
she does not think about
the seduction that trades
her soul for tips.

Symphony in Cordell

I.
In Cordell Oklahoma the highway
circles around the town square

then funnels by the Dollar General
on toward the open grasslands

where men are tempered by empty sky
and sparse land that dares interpretation.

At the diner twelve men take lunch
around jugs of tea, their caps tilted a bit

for leisure – they'll be locked down tight
when they leave – the wind and all.

They wear American denim, high
quality boots, pliers strapped to their belts.

They say *feller* and *holler* and
other words like that.

II.
Two young ladies wait their tables
responsible like a Secretary of State.

They know their business, know how
to talk to these men – these men

who would never take what does not belong
to them, these men who work for fun

whose honor is to avoid being "soft"
who chuckle at the same old jokes.

Will these waitresses stay in Cordell
or will they wind up in the City?

There can't be that many men available
out here but if you needed a wife,

a wife who knows how to talk to men
who knows how to clean up their mess

without offending their egos
tickling their ears while keeping them at bay

like a good hound dog, eager but trainable
floppy skin and a sulky smile,

then these would be your choice
if Cordell were your final stop.

III.
Like the winter wheat around here
these gals are firm, full and green.

Two ruddy pups walk in capped
like their elders, brawny but still tender

as always, life will recycle itself,
and these towns will continue

these folks, bending in the wind,
know better than to long for Eden.

IV.
I pay the bill, climb into my pickup
and circle the square, heading west

rolling red prairies—curious like fate
ominous like time—mark my travel.

On the radio, Haydn's symphony
seems odd at first, but then I listen close,

the venerable movements, the voices
accompany this place, celebrate its life.

One should not be so quick
to make assumptions about Oklahoma.

Cheyenne Meridian

When you get west—
west beyond Cheyenne—
the world curves in on itself
and that is okay by you
because you are at the end
of things yourself
and that too is no matter
because the end
is not a bad place to begin.

I can't think of any place better
to be than here
at the meridian of time and space
earth and sky.

If you drive long enough
or walk prairie dust
sometimes you can't really tell
differences
this mystical meeting
of the imagined
and the known.

Singing in the Kitchen Window

She sang as well as Sammie Smith.
I swear she did. I was fourteen
playing ball in the yard.
Through the open kitchen window
Help me make it through the night
floats in melancholy across the grass
sweet like summer honeysuckle.
A grieving angel washing dishes sings
a beautiful sadness I had not heard before
nor have I rarely heard since.

I had only known her as a happy church pianist
and member of a singing family
talented enough for Nashville.
Even grumpy saints moved to the edge of the pew
when they smiled singing happy hopeful heaven songs.

But on that day these soulful lines:
I don't care what's right or wrong
I won't try to understand
Let the Devil take tomorrow
Lord tonight I need a friend – those lines
froze me in perilous tension:
theological anxiety mixed with raw, sublime emotion.

A short while later their divorce went public
and then I knew the heartsick lady
singing in the kitchen window.

Ramona

Ramona you've been good to me
you're a woman very hard to find
                              -- Rodney Crowell

He knows two women named Ramona.
Wandering from place to place he thinks
he should have married either one of them –
would have too if he could have blended them
together into one flesh at one time.

He drives a big rig, met the first one
waitressing at a truck stop west of Joplin.
Her auburn hair had a way of hanging
around her cheeks when she smiled
placing a platter of chicken fried steak.
She wanted to go to college, she said, but
since high school her dream has been on hold
for quite sometime though she reads
lots of books on her infrequent days off.

The second one danced in a strip club
near Winslow. Her brown skin glowed
in the dark halls where men paid her good money
to forget their memories.

He gave her a ride in his rig and she laughed
right outloud, poked her head out the window
as they pulled through haunted air
climbing toward the Apache Mountains.
She hollered: *I'm riding in a fucking cattle truck*
with Jo Bob and she stuck her arms out
like she was flying to the stars
like she was a star
but when they stopped near Flagstaff,
she had teary eyes and they talked long
into the night about losing dreams.

He runs sometimes five thousand miles a week
when he feels there's nowhere else to go
and only the wheels are his friends
and he knows as he follows familiar routes
that he left them both behind
with only their dreams keeping them sane.

Pickin Up Chicks at Wal-Mart

You don't gotta be cool
you just gotta be there
show yourself
wander through the aisles
through aisle #7, lucky # 7
past briefs, boxers and bras
over to the dog-food
then circle down toward the avocados
pick up speed in the straight-a-way
toward the heartburn medicine
sinus pills and condoms –
all that useless overpriced stuff –
take a right by the cell phones
pause at the TV's and $5 dollar videos
and think about her
think about inviting her to come over
when she finishes getting her hair done
or her tanning session or Bible study
or whatever it is she's got to do –
it's all the same.

It's all her, and she is there –
if you want her, if you can accept
the greening possibility
that you are so normal
you don't even have to shave
to catch the girl of somebody else's dream
like those gals loitering
in the camouflage clothing
thinking about a deer hunter
thinking about a hunt that went wrong.

Nothing says *Git Er Done*
like squeaky wheels on a shopping cart
nothing pulls at her heart like dimming batteries
that need replacing in an old flashlight.

Right after she stocks up on Tyson Chicken
macaroni and cheese, milk, eggs and bread
by God her youngsters won't do without
at least he was always good about that
about getting the child support in –
then he'd limp up the aisle to the fishing tackle
pick up some bobbers and hooks
gotta get ready for crappie season
and *Oh Yeah*, he thinks,
*I need to replace the batteries
in that damn flashlight*

I don't know about you boys
but I don't watch magic shows
for the tricks or because of the magician.
I only watch the beautiful assistants.
That's sleight of hand I can believe.

Good Enough

I live by approximation
perfection has never been my calling
my problems unwind
as I give up absolutes

Absolutely I give up absolutes
and cheer a close second
I used to swing a hammer
framing houses

We're not building cabinets
the boss would holler
Good enough for the girls we go with
we would reply

I am not sure what that means
about me *or* the girls we go with

Framing

We would regard a piece of lumber
like it was a pretty young lady:

soft whistles, raised eye brows, caress it
with our fingertips, say pretty things

about it. Then we would measure her,
mark her and cut her to our precise

dimensions. Then holding her tightly
in place, we would sink sixteen-penny

nails into her solid core with swift
firm hammer strokes, then exclaim

Good Wood! and admire our handiwork
before moving on to the next piece.

Red Dirt and Turquoise

for Jean Marie

She says how much she likes red dirt
You have to hear her say it
The sibilating way she talks
Longing, imploring
The mysteries of red dirt

This land is good for graves
Spirits hovering beyond grassy prairies
Sing about red dirt
A song she's been hearing for sometime now

She wears turquoise
It balances the red dirt
They come from the same core
Her rings her smile her loud honest responses
Honest like the soil of our assumption

Hungarian Men

Thick mustaches drape the dark curves
of wind-beaten faces, some stray hairs
always pointing the wrong way
like the wheat stubble scattered
across the linoleum of Mamma's kitchen

where the farmers sit in wood chairs
that bend under the weight of their Angus-like
shoulders harnessed in grease-stained,
blue-striped overalls powdered in red dust,
their brown eyes hungering for cabbage rolls.

Their forearms lay on the red-checkered
table cloth waiting to draw their battered
hands into their laps and fold their stubby
fingers in prayer to satisfy mamma
while thinking about that *derned old 'Allis*

Chambers' that'll never make it through
harvest and thinking that maybe the hail
will miss them and thinking surely they've
fixed enough fence and thinking mamma
should be about done returning thanks.

Finally "Amen" is said all around
and they grab the nearest dish, working
the utensils as tools feeding themselves
with instinctive pleasure, swallowing hard
followed by regal belches between occasional

guttural words about the sun and rain,
fields and machines, analyzing the parts,
proposing if/then constructions, solving for X,
always solving for the unknown, that is,
after all, how they got to Oklahoma.

Hands

She tells her story
in hesitant phrases, eyes
drooping to consider.

I notice her hands
bigger than mine,
she rubs them like she speaks

Their knobby appearance
braced for the telling,
antique scars unhidden.

Her new young man
married her, planted wheat,
then died before harvest.

She looks up in proud grief,
looks down again
touches the hands as if to comfort

Them for their effort
all those years ago when they
brought in that first harvest

By my own hands
she explains
and planted and harvested

Every season since
for forty years
Just like he'd want me to.

Texoma Morning

Sometimes he notices a breeze
blowing through his open truck window
at sunrise by the river.

He doesn't remember when
or how he first started coming here
to drink beer for breakfast.

He fell into a pattern that is not
without some comfort,
more than a hollow apartment up the road.

He's not seeking anything
–just looking at things:
buzzards loitering, beer cans scattered

Across a sandy beach where fishermen
will soon unload their boats
falling into habits of their own.

Luling Texas

I took a wrong turn
in Luling Texas – didn't mean to—
just missed the sign.

If you take a wrong turn in Luling
you could end up in Seguin
or Schertz or Cibolo
or some damn place unmapped.

Now it might not be such a bad thing
to be lost in a place nobody knows
if that's what you want
but if you have other places to be
well, it's best not to miss a sign.

I was lucky in Luling by the way.
A genuine Samaritan helped me
find my way back.

He didn't just tell me how—no
he started his pickup and led
me back to the right path –
guess he figured some things
are kind of hard to explain.

Roadhouse

green wheat fields
in February

wrinkled trailer houses
windmills

Texas gothic
neon fun:

Show me your tits
leave the judging to God

Lady Liberty blushes
we've lost balance

wheels wobble
but we drive on – following

fallow fields – furtive,
frickin, fruitless freedom

you love the road
you are a road

or at least a goat-path
common to all

Cottonwoods on the Rio Grande

for Richard

You interrupt my sleep
—null my brain waves all day
—your guerilla warfare takes a toll

But I resist
—I look for a faith cast aside
like a shade-tree mechanic looking
for parts in a junk yard

Even if I find it I don't know if it'll run again.

When you hike along a river
—you never know what you'll find
but don't misunderstand:
a drowning man could swim
if the current would not pull him under.

I look up and see a young Bald Eagle
—floating above the Rio Grande
and for a moment, feel this new power
then realize that he is scoping
a small flock of ducks downstream
—and I feel more like a duck these days.
but the Sandia peaks are bold
today in bright sun
—and I refuse despair.

What would it have been like
—to be really wild, living
under Cottonwoods
on this shoreline?

What fate determines who is Native
—and who belongs to Coronado?

I tire of being a wild man:
—Crusoe, Gulliver
and those kind blend to myth.
I want something else now
—even Natty Bumppo knew this.

In my dream an older man
—not unlike myself,
maybe my dad
or maybe myself in advanced years,
leads me down a path
to a peaceful spot on a beautiful river.

He side-steps suddenly
—speaks with careful alarm:
Watch out—Rattlesnake!
Frozen, we watch its enormous length
trail into the underbrush along the road.
We can't see its head
—only the last half of his body
but that is enough to scare us.

We consider following it
—find its head, kill it,
but then we leave it be
—accepting potential danger
accepting things as they are.

I keep thinking about that grove
—of Cottonwoods
the cold water whispering secrets
as it rushes by,
water and sun and orange sand.

The burden of history,
—the weight of truth is on me
as I travel Interstate Forty.
Each run-down settlement we pass
has an abandoned church building,
—yet the stone walls stand.

I think about obligation
—being mayor of your own ghost town.

My friend tells me that carpenters
originally worked with stone,
—so Jesus was a stone mason –
like Socrates. These men thought
—as they touched stone
—as stone touched them,
dust sifting through rough hands
—the hard core holding firm
in a wall they construct
while the mind says
—*Examine and Deny*
—*Examine and Deny*

Like abandoned church walls
these words have yet to erode.

The only fear is betrayal.

My friend also says Judas
was a hairdresser
—thus he knew the secrets of Jesus.

Maybe so
Maybe so.

Silent Trails

for Diane Glancy
after Pushing the Bear

Do you hear their silence
sitting in mourning
on the snowy trail
that takes them far from home
as aliens
stepping along teary destinies?

Their silence
calling out in perilous times
compels us to explain
their apocalypse
slow death wanderings
herded like beasts
wondering what happened to them
what is happening
to their future,
if such a place be imaginable,
if their medicine still works
when the white god deceives them.

Why are they not singing
why not chattering
why must they withdraw
into the purity of objectification?

Their reluctant speech
resounding
in our cold cold hearts
echoing still.

At the Narrows, Mountain Fork River

I met an 87 year-old Choctaw man.

We stood on the low-water bridge
swapping flies, telling tales.

He doesn't wade as much as he
used to – slippery rocks –
he says, but I swear he
is every bit as spry as I ever was.

A returning spirit
he welcomes me to his river –
this One, still walking on water.

Return to the Buffalo River

She never disappoints, this mother
Eden, green with foliage,
white-capped rapids
penetrating mountain hearts.

River of my youth, this sacred place
borders time and turmoil,
restores balance and direction.

My son skips rocks cross-current
as I did so many years ago,
and as I will do again
whenever the need to return
pulls me downstream.

Skipping rocks – that playful game
ancients and moderns share,
a balance of skill and cooperation
with stone, with water – a contest
against yourself, against the river,
against anyone else who wishes
to measure himself
in this timeless game that God made,
the game God plays,
the game boys can never resist.

What Does it Profit a Man?

We discover the 'infinite' and the 'absolute,'
not by straining to escape from the finite
and relative world, but by the most complete
acceptance of its limitations.

—Alan Watts

When Jesus went into the wilderness
familiar strangers met him there,
bargaining for his life.

When you and I went into wilderness
all we found was dark hope
bears and moose and loons

eagles and pike and pines
and granite boulders to sleep on,
water as old as earth.

We laughed in the darkness
disavowing our puritan roots
glad a good god had once gone here too

consoled by summer rain
and homilies voiced in the wind
a holiness unmapped, faith

partnered with timeless rock.
We are well aware of the limits
of earth, of all we see,

of all we know, but in mindfulness
we find something
more than we bargained for.

Mountain Lake

Nine thousand feet high
he mends beside a small camp fire,
pine cones purple in consoling flames.

He blows cigar smoke skyward,
feels stars close enough to touch,
close enough to purge.

His tethered horses rub
against lodgepole pines
reflected in the cutthroat water.

His tent flaps
in the breeze stirring across the lake,
breezes stirring across his soul.

A Blessing

After three days of hard fishing
we lean against the truck
untying boots, removing waders.

We change in silence still feeling
the rhythm of cold water lapping
thankful for that last shoal of rainbows
to soothe the disappointment
of missing a trophy brown.

We'll take with us the communion
of rod and line and bead-head nymphs
sore shoulders and wrinkled feet.

A good tiredness claims us
from slipping over rocks, pushing rapids –
sunup to sundown – sneaking
toward a target, eyes squinting
casting into winter wind.

We case the rods, load our bags
and start to think about dinner.
None of us wants to leave.
None wants to say goodbye.

Winter shadows touch the river cane.
The cold is coming. We look up
into a cobalt sky, and there,
as if an emissary on assignment,
a Bald Eagle floats overhead
close enough to bless us
then swiftly banks sunward
and is gone.

Saturday Night in Austin

Sitting on a Sixth Street bench
Austin slithers, foams around us.

My boy and I talk and listen.
There's a party in every direction,
girls barely dressed
males trying to figure out
how to be men.

Jazz, rock, blues, brats
and onions – unceasing action –
yet we sit as if we're on a quiet gravel bar
on the Buffalo River
counting stars, clarifying dreams
explaining the past, planning the future
living the moments, talking
about life, about cigars, about girls,
about money, sex, and family.

We notice a Nighthawk darting
several stories high
above the oblivious crowd.

I did not know Saturday night in Austin
could be so wild.

Aristotle and His Acorn

He was wrong
about some things
but he was right
about this:

Even in our urbanized
Concretized
technological
mazes,
acorns abound
and oaks remain
possible.

Faith

Faith is not something you wear
like a hat or a new handbag
or even a strong pair of boots and coveralls.

Faith happens when you sit alone
and see morning sun rays
lighten the darkness around you

Until you see the trees individually
each dark trunk, separate green
branches reaching sunward.

Faith is walking through wilderness
seeking nothing but surprises
like a bubbling unmarked spring.

Faith is an act, like turning a radio off
when you're stuck in traffic to let the mind
settle – like water on rock, sunlight in woods.

Mormon Missionaries Pay Me a Visit

I'm sitting on my lawn
enjoying a nice blunt cigar
watching children ride scooters
up and down the street
twilight gently falling,
swallows circling,
Mississippi Kites high overhead,
tree frogs, sounds of sweet shadows

Then I see them in the corner of my eye,
two bikes slow
they can not pass a lost soul –
I'm too conspicuous –
I don't want this feeling, I want them
to pass me by

Good evening sir they say
I'm Elder Hansen says the first
I'm Elder Olson the second chokes
and then they wait
but all I can think to say:
You're kind of young to be elders, aren't you?
They launch into their sales pitch
about Restoration and Heavenly Father
while I recoil in smoke, then interrupt
If I convert do I have to give up this cigar?
They are not sure
but soon get back on track
like a loose wheel wobbling
until they finally bid me good evening.

I watch them roll away
and wonder
what gives them the audacity to interrupt me
while I am at worship.

Security Guard

His skin was perceived
to be too dark.
Guarding the Holocaust Museum

was another flaw.
Preserving a shrine to events
that never happened

threatens white lies.
A pale terrorist rifled
his prey to expunge

delusions of common humanity.
Taking a bullet
for us all proves not only

that the Holocaust occurred,
but for some
it never ended.

A Prayer for Old Men

They should finally go
to peace they've long desired.
Only now are they beginning to see
their pale faces reflected
on the waters
they sit before at sunset.

Unbending, in starched white shirts,
wranglers and hats,
comfortable in narrow boots,
worn lines about their faces
giving way to diminished sparkles
in once proud eyes,
something resembling repentance
occurs to them
in slow stubborn streams.

Listening to wind
moving the waters before them,
now they want peace
though it has taken a lifetime
to give up the manners of war,
to consider that what they've been so sure of,
may have been wrong all along.

Preferring illusions,
they should cross at dusk
when the light has dimmed,
when the peace of growing old
appears gracefully on the waters
in surprising shadows
in voices forgiving in familiar wind.

Then, if they rise again
to discover that their savior is not white
and that god is something
other than a patriarch,
the union may still be kind.

What Pip was Trying to Say

We can't afford to lose whales
by the likes of you
                                   —Stubb

I feel prouder leading thee by thy black
hand, than though I grasped an Emperor's!
                                   —Ahab

Now that we're insane he loves me.

I cost them a whale, but the old man fears
so they can't leave me.
I am salvation to those baptized
in the name of the Devil
ruled by pious capitalism.

Here he comes now
pegging in demonic rhythms.

He tethers me like his pet
his cursed crew cowering toward damnation
distracted only by duty
envious of freedom the insane know.

Poor pagans doomed in the details of duty
realize too late
the sea will have its way.

Our mad father needs me
so they all need me.

I sing their only hope –
dirges in our boat on this sea
where fear lurks on every wave
and wisdom is reduced
to categorical absolutes:
a grand white whale
and a little black cabin boy.

Meeting Ahab

Old Ahab cannot be swayed
to help Captain Gardiner.
His white whale has been spotted
so there is no reasoning,
even begging the Golden Rule
proves futile.

His choice has been made.
His path undeterred.

The Pequod and the Rachel
go separate ways
and our mythology
says Ahab chooses his demise.

We believe this.

But the heart breaks
for the Rachel's absurd fate
drifting in a vast ocean
trying to find a spot of life.
Her suffering only compounded
by the cruel irony of meeting Ahab.

The Rachel bears her loss alone
while the world still asks:
Why is Rachel at the mercy
of Ahab? And why do we
tell ourselves that Ahab's demise
somehow settles a score?

You are responsible Ahab!
For me, for all of us,
but our anguish only seems
to echo the cold, countless waves
unobserved in the belly
of some lost ocean.

These Sharks, Below

Pious harpooners
Never make good voyagers.
—*Peleg in Moby Dick*

Death is always the subject;
only the means are situational.
Beneath the waves,
deep below sight, below senses

Death lurks.
Life is not possible absent this fact.
The one who throws the shaft
must be certain.

There can be no pious distractions,
no fear about death.
Prophets and executioners
know the heart.

They share a stage with God.
They travel with us.
We look out over the vast sea
and guess our end.

We rebel against Grace
settle for piety
for pointless rules,
pretending the soul needs a line,

denying the fiddler his tune,
ourselves the dance.
When great death hunts you
will the shark be in you?

Streaking at Bible Camp

in Mexico's mountains
pure wild bliss

   aplomb

the hope of heaven
after a crisp shower

  – Why not? –

you rejoiced across camp
in front of the youth pastor
and other neophytes

the puritans, of course,
made it a sin

and you were asked to leave

but in your expulsion
you brought something back
they will never know

and God, sitting cross-legged
on a sunny hillside
among the firs
beyond the tabernacle
laughed right out loud
gently tapped his thigh
and whispered
well done, My Son,
well done.

Summer Rain

At the cabin
  where a native creek cuts flint
  and limestone, white foam bubbles
  in slack water, sycamore and
  birch hold an eroding bank,
  cane and mint before bluestem
  and parched flowers

A sultry day
  so hot, so humid even believers
  doubt before July thunder finally
  fires bullet-like rain drops,
  few and fierce at first, then
  a full-throttled onslaught
  the sun recedes

A sincere man
  frees himself fulfilling a life-long
  impulse, disrobes and dances
  like a delirious bear naked
  in the rain, his humble white
  pot-bellied flesh praising
  gods of summer

In the dark trees
  Vireos, warblers and all manner
  of songbirds wink in approval
  nod to each other trying their best
  not to laugh while celebrating
  this all-too-human assault
  on modesty

Shine on, Brother: A Tribute to Balding Men

They shall not make baldness
upon their head
– Leviticus

So what do you got against us bald guys anyway?
You think we're responsible for letting the Snake loose?
You blame us because Eve had a change in taste of wardrobe
while Adam and the Old Man played hide and seek?

Come on, look at us! Behold our pathetic, smooth
fleshy foreheads with ever-expanding scalps.
How can such diminished creatures determine anything?

Scandalized by heritage,
despised by culture
excommunicated by hairy saints
ridiculed by children
ignored by Eve's daughters

Can't you see sublimity in our halos?

Maybe our bald affinity with flesh
is too intimidating for those praying to never be exposed.

Oh Eve, you don't have to hide any more.
If you only realized how passé fig leaves really are,
If you only knew, like us, the bliss
of accepting your good naked self.

Eve's Daughters—
or How the Snake Overplayed his Hand

You know Cain and Abel
but did you know that Eve also had two daughters?

Call them Miranda #1 and Miranda #2
(the original names are lost in translation).

Miranda #1 can be a real psycho-bitch;
theologians and feminists debate
whether this is the fault of mom or dad.

All I know is that she is waaaaay
too much like her brother.

Miranda #2 is not like her sister at all.
She adores her parents, especially mom
(which gives the feminists ammunition
in their argument with the theologians).

She wants nothing more than to please
get good grades and maybe one day
be Secretary of State or run for President
and if that doesn't work out,
she still has her waitressing job.

One day the Snake shows up
at their apartment and starts telling lies
about their mother,
how she had screwed everything up,
how she had caused her man –
and the world – untold grief.

The Mirandas look at each other wondering
"Can this be true" they ask Snake?

"Damn straight" says Snake.
"I wouldn't lie to you."

Then Miranda #1 looks at Miranda #2
and they share a knowing grin.

If a snake wouldn't lie,
then there is nothing to believe in
and certainly nothing to fear.

Genesis

I.
In the beginning
God created
and ever since
we've all been imitating
immortality
hoping words can reach depths
of pure darkness
plumb the high crystal stars
with imagination.

Poets are especially bad about this.

If God is anything like love
then that matters most
and all our words, all our patterns
follow something we feel inside
something we desperately want to bring to life.

You hear us rant about injustice
and pain and all nuances of history.
You put up with our clever comic attempts
but all this is just longing
for love, for absolute love.

II.
A man went to visit an old friend.
She was now old. Someday she would die.
They both knew that.

Her face was drawn like a cross.

Do you know how hard I've tried
to not be old? Do you know how hard
that is? To not be old?
Her smile was like a drying creek bed in August.

But I wanted more! Something more.
Just because I am old it doesn't mean
I don't feel. That I don't desire.
You know?
I want to feel. Don't want to give that up
the tingle, the possibility. You know?

As she spoke he lay down beside her
in her old bed and propped her tender head
beneath his own aging arms
gathered her close
like flowers, careful not to tarnish petals
careful to breathe these moments together.

And they knew then
what poets and people want most
and he knew that words are just things
and images are but gravel
stones in a stream bed
billions of pieces of rock
over which streams of water pass.

Hospice

*for Jake
and those who know, love,
live with dying*

the sadness that I knew you
swings
on the empty porch
summer's breeze
half-filled glasses of dark beer
quaint railroad tracks
crossing
nameless new neighbors
where trains no longer go
dusty canoe and rusty bikes
hung
loosely in a garage
where paint cans
dribbled
obsolete colors
weld
a cracked concrete canvas
too familiar
       to notice
too common
       to christen
too sad
       to ignore

Book People

In a dark paneled room
brown shelves stacked full
beside a dim lamp

plants hang on to green
in once brightly-painted pots
bought years ago

a few dead leaves scattered
among books, papers and the trinkets
that have made them

and that still comfort them
by sheer familiarity
appeasing dreams yet to be known.

Of good books there is no end,
never time enough
to contemplate all the thoughts

that would parade before their imagination,
a futile dance between themselves
and the eternity of art.

They sit in subdued tones
hushed in a place where hope
still rises at the turning of a page

by the shaded windows,
evening sun filtered
through dusty blinds half-pulled

a sweating cup of tea
rings on the closest shelf,
a silence too strong for fear.

Nightfall

The second longest night
of the year falls to silence.
Layers of blue sky darken
beyond bare Oak limbs
against a somber pink horizon.

A vacant bird feeder stands
in the cold dusk, chimney
smoke curls down outside,
orange coals glow inside
inviting reflection:

The family is scattered now
like a frightened covey,
but memories prevail
despite fragmentation,
despite the illusions.

Hollow red and green bulbs
blink off and on, an image
reflecting in the bay window
reminding of loss while
evoking renewal.

The Magi frozen in time
on the fireplace mantel echo
unfulfilled quests. There is
something holy in losing,
something sacred in memory –

When birth and death,
nature and humanity are considered,
when the parts and the whole
come together – at least for these
solstitial moments.

Groundwork

The end of art is peace
                                    –Seamus Heaney

If you must turn ground
by hand, then so be it

that is what you must do.
This is what you can give

and some will receive it,
plant seeds in furrows

you make and wait
for full fruition,

a harvest that comes
incrementally,

one new hand at a time.
While cynics scoff

of idealism and warn
of recurring pain

what choice do we have
but to plow and plant?

Ken Hada is a fourth-generation Oklahoman, descendant of Danish and Hungarian immigrants: Gypsy poets, barn dance aficionados, art lovers, amateur philosophers, wheat farmers, preachers, teachers and common-sense craftsmen. Ken claims northwest Oklahoma and the Ozarks as his homes, though he readily embraces the natural world wherever he travels. Much of his free time finds him walking prairies, ascending small mountains, flyfishing and kayaking native streams, the Gulf Coast or Canadian lakes. Ken completed his PhD at The University of Texas in Arlington, writing on Cormac McCarthy's *Border Trilogy*. Since 2000, he has been a professor at East Central University in Ada, Oklahoma where he teaches American literatures and courses in the humanities. He also directs the annual Scissortail Creative Writing Festival held each April at ECU. He authored a chapbook of link poems with Japanese translation in conjunction with Ogaki Women's College in 1994. His collection, *The Way of the Wind*, was published in 2008 by Village Books Press. Much of his creative writing and critical research blends in the area of nature writing, ecocriticism, and regional "people's history." He serves as area chair for Literature: Ecocriticism and the Environment for the annual Popular Culture Association meeting held in Albuquerque. Some of his interpretive writing appears in *College Literature, Southwestern American Literature, Ethnic Studies Review, American Indian and Culture Research Journal, Journal of the West, Papers on Language and Literature* and *Journal of American Studies Association of Texas*.

CPSIA information can be obtained
at www.ICGtesting.com
Printed in the USA
LVHW041721040219
606320LV00003B/694/P

9 780980 168440